Family Life

6

STUDENT EDITION

David Thomas, PhD

General Editor

RCL Benziger®

Cincinnati, Ohio

The Subcommittee on the Catechism, United States Conference of Catholic Bishops, has found this text, copyright 2011, to be in conformity with the *Catechism of the Catholic Church*; it may be used only as supplemental to other basal catechetical texts.

Consultants

Paul Duckro, PhD
Tim Hogan, PsyD
Tom Everson
Fanny Pedraza

NIHIL OBSTAT
Rev. Msgr. Robert Coerver
Censor Librorum

IMPRIMATUR
† Most Reverend Kevin J. Farrell DD
Bishop of Dallas

May 3, 2010

The *Nihil Obstat* and *Imprimatur* are official declarations that the material reviewed is free of doctrinal or moral error. No implication is contained therein that those granting the *Nihil Obstat* and *Imprimatur* agree with the contents, opinions, or statements expressed.

Send all inquiries to:
RCL Benziger
8805 Governor's Hill Drive • Suite 400
Cincinnati, Ohio 45249

Toll Free   877-275-4725
Fax   800-688-8356

Visit us at www.RCLBenziger.com/FamilyLife

20656   ISBN 978-0-7829-1506-8 (Student Edition)
20666   ISBN 978-0-7829-1516-7 (Parent Connection)
20686   ISBN 978-0-7829-1536-5 (Teacher Edition)

6th printing.
Manufactured for RCL Benziger in Cincinnati, OH, USA.
October 2013.

RCL Benziger Development Team

James Spurgin
Editor

Tricia Legault
Design

Laura Fremder
Production

Daniel S. Mulhall
National Catechetical Advisor

Jo Rotunno
Director of Catechist and Professional Development

Susan Smith
Director of Project Development

Ed DeStefano
Publisher

Peter M. Esposito
President

ACKNOWLEDGMENTS

Excerpts from the *New American Bible* with Revised New Testament and Revised Psalms © 1991, 1986, 1970 Confraternity of Christian Doctrine, Washington, D.C. and are used by permission of the copyright owner. All Rights Reserved. No part of the New American Bible may be reproduced in any form without permission in writing from the copyright owner.

PHOTO CREDITS

Cover, UpperCut Images/Punchstock; Page 5, Michael Newman/Photoedit; 8, NBAE/Gettyimages; 9, Radius Images/Gettyimages; 11, OJO Images/Gettyimages; 12, Gerard Fritz/Gettyimages; 14, Gene Plaisted, OSC/The Crosiers; 15, Mike Kemp/Gettyimages; 16, Rubberball/Punchstock; 18, Gene Plaisted, OSC/The Crosiers; 21, SuperStock; 22, Kevin Dodge/Corbis; 23, C Devan/Corbis; 24, SW Productions/Gettyimages; 27, Bettmann/Corbis; 28, Pixland/SuperStock; 30, Paintings by Terrance J. Nelson/Minneapolis, MN; 33, Michael Newman/Photoedit; 34, Blend Images/Punchstock; 35, Karen Knauer/Gettyimages; 36, Steve Allen/Alamy; 39, Chip Mitchell/Gettyimages; 39, Nathan Schepker/iStock; 40; Ariel Skelley/Gettyimages; 42, Gene Plaisted, OSC/The Crosiers; 45, Lisa F. Young/iStock; 46, Blend Images/Punchstock; 47, Radius Images/SuperStock; 48, InspireStock Images/Fotosearch; 48, Radius Images/Punchstock; 48, SuperStock; 48, Corbis Photography/Veer; 50, The Art Archive/Cobis; 51, Gale Zucker/Gettyimages; 52, Catherine Yeulet/iStock; 52, Jim West/Photoedit; 52, SuperStock; 54, Gene Plaisted, OSC/The Crosiers; 57, Creatas/Punchstock; 58, Getty Images/Gettyimages; 59, Thinkstock/Gettyimages; 60, Jupiterimages/Gettyimages; 62, Apis/Sygma/Corbis; 63, Bettmann/Corbis; 64, WP Wittman; 64, WP Wittman; 66, The order of the Most Holy Trinity

CONTENTS

The Catholic Home

Unit 1: God's Gift of Family

Unit 2: God's Gift of Self

Unit 3: God's Gift of Life

Unit 4: God's Gift of Love

Unit 5: God's Gift of Community

Reviewing Grade 6

The Catholic Home

Life in Christ

In Baptism, you have been called to share in the life of Christ. You have been given a great gift, but the gift requires that you give your best effort to follow Christ. This means that you need to learn the difference between right and wrong and choose to do what is right and good. When you learn to choose to do what is right, you are leading a life in Christ.

The following list will help you review how to lead a life in Christ. Almost everything you will learn this year has been designed to help you and your family love your way through life, by following the way of Jesus. In these ways, you can share a family life in Christ:

1. **You have been created in the image and likeness of God.** This truth is the starting point for Christian living in a Catholic home.

2. **You are called to do what is good.** The Ten Commandments and the Beatitudes tell you that God calls you to live a healthy, holy and happy life. Being weakened by the effects of Original Sin makes doing what is good difficult. With God's grace you can choose good.

3. **You are created to be happy.** You have a natural desire to be happy. The Church teaches that when you know, love and serve God, you can be truly happy.

4. **You are created free.** You have the gift of free will. This makes it possible to choose how to live and to act. Yet God calls you to be responsible for your actions.

5. **You have a conscience.** You have the ability to know the difference between what is right and what is wrong. This judgment is called *conscience*. The Sacred Scriptures, the teachings of the Catholic Church and the examples of the saints and other good people help you to inform and form your conscience and follow it.

6. **You have been given the gifts of the virtues.** At your Baptism, you were given the gifts of faith, hope and love. These Theological Virtues help you to develop all the good habits you need to live in Christ. With God's grace, you can live according to the virtues.

7. **The Holy Spirit helps you lead a good life.** Jesus sent the Holy Spirit into the world to help people, including you, to lead a healthy, holy and happy life.

8. **God is merciful.** God gives the gift of mercy to all those who are sorry for their sins, receive the Sacraments and strive to do what is good. When we sin, we fail to love God and others. Yet we can, with God's merciful and forgiving love, change our ways.

9. **You have a responsibility to the human community.** You have been made to live in community. You are called to help society live according to the way of Jesus.

10. **You follow legitimate authority.** Inspired by the Holy Spirit, the Church helps you learn about Christian living. You follow the authority of the Pope and the bishops. You follow the just rules of society. And most importantly, you obey your parents.

11. **You have the Ten Commandments and the Beatitudes as your guide.** Learning to follow the Ten Commandments and to live in the spirit of the Beatitudes will help you love your way through a life in Christ.

12. **You know and follow the law of love.** In everything you do, you want to show that you love God with your whole heart and that you love your neighbor as yourself.

Prayers for the Family

The Sign of the Cross

In the name of the Father,
and of the Son,
and of the Holy Spirit.
Amen.

The Lord's Prayer

Our Father, who art in heaven,
hallowed be thy name;
thy kingdom come;
thy will be done
    on earth as it is in heaven.
Give us this day our daily bread,
and forgive us our trespasses
as we forgive those who trespass against us;
And lead us not into temptation,
but deliver us from evil. Amen.

Glory Be

Glory be to the Father
and to the Son
and to the Holy Spirit,
as it was in the beginning
is now and ever shall be
world without end. Amen.

Prayer to the Holy Spirit

Come, Holy Spirit, fill the hearts of your faithful.
And kindle in them the fire of your love.
Send forth your Spirit and they shall be created.
And you will renew the face of the earth.
Lord,
by the light of the Holy Spirit
you have taught the hearts of your faithful.
In the same Spirit
help us to relish what is right
and always rejoice in your consolation.
We ask this through Christ our Lord. Amen.

The Hail Mary

Hail Mary, full of grace,
the Lord is with thee.
Blessed art thou among women,
and blessed is the fruit
    of thy womb, Jesus.
Holy Mary, Mother of God,
pray for us sinners,
now, and at the hour of our death.
Amen.

Morning Prayer

Almighty God, you have given us this day.
Strengthen us with your power and keep us from falling into sin.
So that whatever we say or think or do may be in your service,
and for the sake of your kingdom. Amen.

Evening Prayer

Lord, watch over us this night.
By your strength, may we rise at daybreak to rejoice
in the Resurrection of Christ, your Son,
who lives and reigns forever and ever. Amen.

A Vocation Prayer

God our Father, it is your will that all people be saved and come
to the knowledge of the truth. Send workers into your great harvest
that the Gospel might be preached to every person, and that your
people, gathered together by the Word of Life and strengthened
by the power of the Sacraments, may advance in the way of
Salvation and love. Grant this through Christ our Lord. Amen.

Family Prayer

Heavenly Father, you have given us a beautiful example in the
Holy Family of Jesus, Mary and Joseph. Give us openness to your
Spirit, so that we may follow through in the practice of virtues.
Strengthen our bonds of love. Grant us the courage to reach out
to those in need and to do your will. Amen.

Family Living

The Corporal Works of Mercy

Feed the hungry.
Give drink to the thirsty.
Give clothes to those who have none.
Shelter the homeless.
Visit the sick.
Visit the imprisoned.
Bury the dead.

The Spiritual Works of Mercy

Help the sinner.
Teach the ignorant.
Counsel the doubtful.
Comfort the sorrowful.
Bear wrongs patiently.
Forgive injuries.
Pray for the living and the dead.

Ten Commandments

1. I am the Lord your God: you shall not have strange gods before me.
2. You shall not take the name of the Lord your God in vain.
3. Remember to keep holy the Lord's Day.
4. Honor your father and your mother.
5. You shall not kill.
6. You shall not commit adultery.
7. You shall not steal.
8. You shall not lie.
9. You shall not covet your neighbor's wife.
10. You shall not covet your neighbor's goods.

Based on Exodus 20:2–3, 7–17

The Beatitudes

Blessed are the poor in spirit,
    for theirs is the kingdom of heaven.
Blessed are they who mourn,
    for they will be comforted.
Blessed are the meek,
    for they will inherit the land.
Blessed are they who hunger
        and thirst for righteousness,
    for they will be satisfied.

Blessed are the merciful,
    for they will be shown mercy.
Blessed are the clean of heart,
    for they will see God.
Blessed are the peacemakers,
    for they will be called children of God.
Blessed are they who are persecuted
        for the sake of righteousness,
    for theirs is the kingdom of heaven.

Matthew 5:3–10

The Apostles' Creed

I believe in God,
the Father almighty,
creator of heaven and earth,
and in Jesus Christ, his only Son, our Lord,
who was conceived by the Holy Spirit,
born of the Virgin Mary,
suffered under Pontius Pilate,
was crucified, died and was buried;
he descended into hell;
on the third day he rose again from the dead;
he ascended into heaven,
and is seated at the right hand
  of the God the Father almighty;
from there he will come again
  to judge the living and the dead.
I believe in the Holy Spirit,
the holy catholic Church,
the communion of saints,
the forgiveness of sins,
the resurrection of the body,
and life everlasting. Amen.

The Theological Virtues
Faith, Hope and Love

The Cardinal Virtues
Justice, Fortitude, Temperance, Prudence

UNIT 1
God's Gift of Family

The Value of Life

The dignity of every person is rooted in the reality that each person has been created in the image and likeness of God. The great diversity among individuals and peoples manifests the beauty, wonder and goodness of God. Our uniqueness is not primarily in our DNA. It is rooted in our uniqueness as individual persons created and gifted by God.

Contemporary science focuses our individual uniqueness in our genes, in our DNA. Increasing knowledge of the genetic structure of plants, animals and humans provides the opportunity to seek cures for disease. For example, there are over two thousand diseases or conditions linked to genes.

Using science without a solid valuing of human life violates the dignity of the human person and is contrary to the divine plan of Creation. We are called to respect every human life at all stages of development. Every person, regardless of their physical abilities or disabilities, possesses sacred value.

Family Blessings

Lord, we are all one in you. How wonderful you have created us, beautiful in our uniqueness and strong in our connectedness. Amen.

Healthy Habits in the Home

Trace the family's traits and traditions through a genogram or family tree. Include physical characteristics, such as height and color of eyes and hair, as well as personal achievements and ethnic and religious celebrations.

Taking the Lesson Home

Learn from your family history through images and stories. Take what you have learned and discussed as a family to draw up a plan for preserving family memories in a digital photo album or the like.

As a family, talk about each statement:

1. How far back can we trace our family name?

2. From which continents and countries do our ancestors come?

3. What are the religious customs and traditions celebrated by our family?

4. What adversities has our family overcome?

5. What might we say about the future of our family?

Making Connections

To help your family learn about its history, invite family members to spend time together and share responses to each of these questions:

▶ Which traits have I inherited from my parents?

▶ Which traits do we see that we share in common?

▶ What new family traditions have we begun?

Faith on the Fridge

The genealogy of every person
is a life of mystery
in truth and love
(based on Blessed Pope John Paul II's
Letter to Families 9).

Family
Web Time
RCLBFamilyLife.com

Connected to the Past

Adam Divac had just walked in when he saw his dad staring intently at the television. "Thank God, I thought we'd never see this day," his father said. "See what?" Adam asked. "What's all the excitement about?" His father said with tears in his eyes, "A cease-fire has just been declared in Kosovo. Maybe the killing will stop now."

The next day in school, Adam and his classmates stood looking at a world map. "I still didn't get it," Adam told his friends. "I was thinking, I'm glad there's a cease-fire, but why cry about it? I guess my dad could see I was puzzled because he went on to explain it to me. 'What happens in Kosovo is important to us,' he told me. 'Your great-grandparents came from there. The people in Kosovo are our people. They belong to us. They share our family traditions. That's why we care when something like this happens.'"

"How many of you know where your family came from?" the teacher asked. "Your ethnicity is really more than race or nationality. It includes the customs, or ways of doing things, that are handed on from one generation to the next."

The class then discussed the great diversity of people in the United States of America. "Our diversity is what makes our nation strong," the teacher pointed out. "But sometimes it also leads to prejudice and other issues that divide people."

Knowing your family roots helps you understand who you are and what you share with past generations. When you appreciate your own roots, you can appreciate the traditions of others too. That's when all people can learn to cooperate with one another. That's when any divisions can be overcome as we recognize our common humanity.

> **This lesson will help you to:**
> - **explore** how your family's background shapes you.
> - **appreciate** the diversity God created among families.
> - **discover** some of your personal gifts and choose to use them.

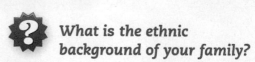

What is the ethnic background of your family?

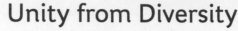

Catholics Believe

Jesus gave the Apostles the mission to make people of all nations his disciples. The Church today continues to be made up of a diversity of peoples with a great diversity of gifts. The Church is one because all her members are joined to Christ in Baptism as the one Body of Christ.

Unity from Diversity

America has been described as a melting pot. In the 1800s and 1900s, people came to the United States mainly from Europe. They wanted to become part of this new homeland. During the last two hundred years both the government and the Church encouraged the Americanization of immigrants. The result was a blending together of many ethnic groups.

Today the United States is more of a salad bowl than a melting pot. In a salad, many different kinds of vegetables, fruits and other ingredients can be tossed together. They keep their identity and at the same time combine to make something new. Every ingredient brings its own flavor to make the new mix.

The United States is made up of many ethnic groups. This combining has added its own flavor to the United States. Various regions of the country have developed customs of their own. New Orleans, for example, has its own uniqueness while New England has another. California has a distinct approach to living that differs from the style of Minnesota or Kansas.

Families across the United States contribute their own ethnic heritage and style, blending it with the general culture wherever they live. Families also create their own unique customs, unrelated to their ethnic backgrounds. For example, some families enjoy a pancake breakfast every Saturday morning. Others enjoy walking their dog.

 Think about some of the unique activities that your family does every week or each year.

Some families are made up of diverse ethnic cultures. For example, a family whose descendants were from Ireland might adopt a son from Thailand and a daughter from Brazil. These families blend and celebrate a variety of customs and traditions that reflect their own unique way of living. From the diversity of families, we draw strength, helping us to appreciate and honor our own family heritage.

Individual Differences

Just as every family is unique, so is every individual, every member of a family. God created each person to be unique with different and wonderful gifts. These diverse gifts reflect the diversity within creation. When you see people of many backgrounds together, you can see the beauty of God's diverse creation.

As you grow older, you will continue some family customs and leave others behind. The influence of your family will remain strong in you. If you marry and have children, you and your spouse will bring together your family backgrounds. Together you will decide which ethnic, social, cultural and religious customs you will continue to make part of your new family.

Growing in Virtue

Reverence is seeing and respecting the dignity and God-given differences of individuals and of peoples. When you respect the traditions of your family, you show reverence for the diversity that God created among all families.

"Family Guidebook"

Make an outline of a family guidebook. List the various ethnic, social, cultural and religious celebrations and activities that occur in your family.

Catholic Family Album

The people of the Church have many customs that help our families grow in faith, hope and love. Among these are popular devotions celebrated by the whole Church and those celebrated only by a certain group of people. Devotion to the **Infant Jesus of Prague** is a popular devotion to the baby Jesus that began either in Spain or in Czechoslovakia in the 17th century. This popular image represents the diverse cultural influences in prayerful devotions to Christ. Today this devotion to the Infant Jesus of Prague is celebrated by Catholics around the world.

Using Your Gifts

Some people have the gift of great intelligence. Others have the gift to make wise decisions. Others have terrific athletic abilities. Some have the gift of telling funny jokes. You might have a friend who is easy to talk with and outgoing.

God has blessed each of us (that includes you) with many gifts. All gifts have a purpose. They benefit the human family by bringing joy and meaning to you and to others. Some of your gifts will also help you relate to others, earn a living and make the world a better place.

Use this checklist to help you discover some of your gifts and talents. Mark the sentence with a 1 if it fits you just right, a 2 if it only fits in some ways and a 3 if it doesn't fit you at all.

__I care about people.

__I like to work alone.

__I am comfortable listening to people's problems.

__I like being at the center of things.

__I like working "behind the scenes."

__I like being with children.

__I enjoy helping out at Mass.

__I like to read.

__I like to organize events.

__I am interested in how the human body works.

__I like solving math problems.

__I like making people laugh.

__I am interested in astronomy.

__I like animals.

__I like to learn how a computer works.

__I like taking things apart.

__I am curious.

__I like to sing.

__I like to be outdoors.

__I am a good speaker.

__I enjoy having quiet time alone to pray.

__I like to figure things out.

__I like to do things a new way.

Look over how you have rated your gifts.

- What do those you marked with 1 say about you?
- How have you been using your gifts to help others up to now?
- How might the list help you know your vocation or career in the future?

Choose one of your gifts. Tell how you will use it in the next few days.

Family Traits

Your Personal Blueprint

A blueprint is an essential tool when a new building is being planned. It is a designer's picture of how a new building will be structurally built. A blueprint shows the size and shape of the building and the number and arrangement of rooms. It indicates the position of features such as doors, windows, closets and appliances. The builder uses the blueprint to construct the building according to the designer's plan.

God has created you to be unique—the only you he will ever create. There will never be another you. Your physical nature is revealed through your physical "blueprint" in your genetic makeup. At the first moment of your life, when you were conceived in your mother's womb, you acquired your genetic "blueprint." This is part of God's plan for human beings. The size and shape of your body, the color and shape of your eyes, the color and texture of your hair and many other physical attributes about you were put in place. Science helps us see what God has created.

The building blocks of your body are cells. Your body is made of billions of cells. Each cell contains a nucleus surrounded by cytoplasm. The nucleus of each cell also contains chromosomes. Under a microscope, a chromosome looks like a transparent thread with tiny "beads" clinging to it. Those beads are genes. Altogether there are one hundred thousand genes in each cell.

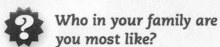

Who in your family are you most like?

The genes that influence who you are physically tell something about your physical heritage as well. Your genetic makeup is based on that of your parents. They, in turn, received theirs from your grandparents, who received theirs from your great grandparents. Your genetic code connects back many generations.

> This lesson will help you to:
> - **recognize** God's plan in our genetic makeup.
> - **understand** the uniqueness of the individual.
> - **identify** and decide to use personality traits to help your family.

Genetics

Genetics, the study of genes, helps explain how people have particular physical traits. Genetics shows that gender is determined at the moment of conception. If you are male, every cell in your body contains a pair of chromosomes called XY. If you are female, every cell in your body contains a pair of chromosomes called XX. Other traits are set by your genetic makeup as well.

Individual physical traits are influenced by both dominant and recessive genes. The gene for brown eyes, for example, is dominant, or stronger, than the gene for blue eyes. The gene for blue eyes is a recessive gene. Whenever two different genes are passed on for the same trait, the dominant gene usually "wins." This simply means it prevents the recessive gene from showing its traits.

Sometimes genes can also give features that are a combination of recessive and dominant qualities. Occasionally two recessive genes are stronger than one dominant gene. If your mother has curly hair and your father has straight hair, you might have wavy hair. The same thing can happen with the color of your skin. Your own skin coloring can be a blend of both of your parents' coloring.

 Think about some of the traits that you share with your family.

Body and Soul

You are far more than your physical traits. God has created you not only with a body but also with a soul. You have an intellect and a free will. God has given you the ability to discern, or come to know, the traits, talents and gifts he has given to you. He has given you the ability to freely choose to use those gifts not only for your own benefit but also for the benefit of others. For example, if a person has a talent for science and math, they may choose to become a doctor, an engineer or perhaps a math teacher. God has given you the freedom and responsibility to discern how to best use your gifts.

Seeking the advice and assistance of family members may help you to plan and attain your own goals for the future. What you do with your talents is up to you.

Growing in Virtue

Your physical traits do not determine the quality of your life. God has given you the **responsibility** to freely choose how to use your gifts. Use responsibly those gifts for your own benefit as well as for the benefit of others.

"Tracing Your Traits"

List dominant and recessive traits in your family that you have inherited or imagine what traits your children might inherit from you.

Dominant Traits	Recessive Traits

Catholic Family Album

Saint Albert the Great (1206–1280) was a scientist, philosopher and theologian who lived in Germany. Albert believed and knew that all things come from God. He sought the truth from a variety of sources including Greek and Arab thinkers. Like Thomas Aquinas, his student, Albert taught that science and faith, theologians and scientists, could work together to come to a deeper understanding of God and creation. In 1931 the Catholic Church recognized him as both a Saint and a Doctor of the Church.

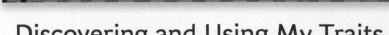

Discovering and Using My Traits

Your genes carry a kind of code that spells out many of your physical traits. Decode the traits listed on the chart by unscrambling the letters. Circle any that describe you. Then answer the questions at the end.

DECODING YOUR TRAITS

Personality

ERISSOU	HSY	AUTCSIOU
OMPASSCEIONAT	GRESAGESIV	UTGOGOIN
ERVNSOU	ACML	ARDGIN

Talents

THLACETI	USIMLCA	ERVLBA
RAMDCATI	RTIACSTI	EADELPRSHI
RGANIZOLATIONA	ECHAMLNICA	REACETIV

1. Of which trait are you most proud?

_____

2. Which, if any, would you like to change? Why?

_____

3. Which do you hope to develop or to use someday?

_____

4. Describe how you will use one trait to help your family today.

_____

Name ....

Summary

Remember what you have learned in each of the lessons in God's Gift of Family.

LESSON 1: Family Background

• I am shaped by my family's history, customs and faith.

• Ethnic diversity gives my family and each family strength and richness.

• When I respect the traditions of my family, I show reverence for the diversity and variety that God created among all families.

LESSON 2: Family Traits

• My genetic makeup does not determine the quality of my life.

• Science and faith complement each other in understanding God, ourselves and creation.

• God has given me the responsibility to discern and use the gifts he has given me not only for my own good but also for the good of my family and the good of others.

Thinking It Through

1. Why is learning about your family important?

_____

_____

_____

2. Which family activity, custom or tradition would tell something important about your family?

_____

_____

_____

3. What difference can your family make in your neighborhood? In the Church?

_____

_____

_____

Matching It Up

On each line, write the letter of the description in Column B that best goes with the term in Column A.

A

1. ....Dominant

2. ....Ethnicity

3. ....Genetics

4. ....Heredity

5. ....Reverence

B

A. Showing honor or respect

B. Refers to all the traits and characteristics a person inherits

C. Ways of doing things that are handed on from one generation to the next

D. Genes that prevent the others from showing their traits

E. The scientific study of genes

Name ....

Recalling Key Concepts

Circle the T if the statement is true. Circle the F if the statement is false.

1. Your ethnic background influences you.   T   F
2. Every person is unique and is created in God's image and likeness.   T   F
3. Diversity adds richness and challenges to family life.   T   F
4. Your genetic makeup is only related to dominant genes.   T   F
5. Your physical traits determine the quality of your life.   T   F

Fill in the missing words in these sentences.

6. From our .... we draw strength, helping us to appreciate and honor our own family.

7. From the moment of ...., you existed as a unique and sacred person.

8. Over the last century, both the government and the Church encouraged the

   ...., or the blending together, of diverse ethnic groups in the United States.

9. Today the culture of the United States is more of a .... than a melting pot.

10. Individual traits are the result of interaction by dominant and recessive ....

Working Together

In a small group, read Genesis 37:3 and create your own Joseph's coat of many colors to represent your group. Use stripes of different colors, textures, patterns, etc. for the various traits of the group. Display your coat of diversity. Spend time at home to work together to create a family Joseph's coat.

God's Gift of Self

Running Toward God

Saul was a young man who knew what he was after. He thought, as a committed Jew, his vocation was to use his gifts and talents to stamp out the growth of Christianity in the first century. One day Saul was traveling earnestly toward Damascus with arrest warrants for the Christians living there. Suddenly, he was stopped in his tracks by the voice of Jesus (see Acts of the Apostles 9:1–9). That extraordinary experience guided Saul, who now is known by his Roman name, Paul.

From then on, Paul had a new understanding of his vocation. Using those same gifts and talents, Paul worked single-mindedly for Jesus Christ by spreading the Gospel. At the end of his life, Saint Paul looked back on his life and knew that he had honestly and faithfully worked at fulfilling the vocation he had received. He had accomplished the work God had given him to do. He wrote, "I have competed well; I have finished the race; I have kept the faith" (2 Timothy 4:7).

Family Blessings

Come, Holy Spirit, strengthen us with your grace to face with courage the challenges in life, to attain our goals even beyond our needs and to work faithfully to reach our final goal of everlasting life with you, the Father, and the Son. Amen.

Healthy Habits in the Home

Spend time together as a family identifying and planning some short-term and long-term goals for the family. Build the goals on the talents and traits of the members of your family. Be sure to include input from each family member and assign responsibility to each as well.

The Conversion of St. Paul, c.1601
Michelangelo Merisi da Caravaggio (1571–1610 Italian)

Taking the Lesson Home

Establish family goals by asking the following questions of each other. Then discuss how to achieve these goals.

What are our goals in regards to:

1. family time?

2. prayer?

3. service?

4. enjoyment?

5. education?

Making Connections

Help your family plan for the future. Have family members respond to and share ideas about each of these questions:

▶ What past experiences have taught you about yourself?

▶ How have you dealt with past failures?

▶ Who has helped you along the way in achieving your goals?

Faith on the Fridge

The Christian family is a sign of the Holy Trinity. It is a sign of the love of One God in Three Divine Persons—God the Father, God the Son and God the Holy Spirit.

Family Web Time
RCLBFamilyLife.com

Creativity at Work

Imagine that X marks where you are right now in your life. You know about your family background. You inherited a genetic package. You have an ethnic, social, cultural and religious background. At this point in your life, you might also have some ideas about your future. But all of this information still does not fully explain who you are.

One important thing to understand is that you are changing all the time. In fact, you will be changing for the rest of your life. You will always be learning about yourself, about life and about God's plan for you.

You bring a unique perspective and your own style to everything you do. As you mature, everything you do affects yourself and the people around you. The world is waiting for you to make your contribution!

The gift of creativity enables you to explore and develop different ways of doing things. Your creativity can help you choose where you are going in life. All along the way, your creativity flows from the unique person you are. Your use of this gift is as unique as your thumbprint—no two people use it in exactly the same way.

God desires that you use all of your gifts and talents in a loving and good way. Maybe you will be the one to discover a medical breakthrough in cancer research or maybe you will find a creative way to reach out to a lonely person.

Learn to use your creativity to deal with people, make decisions and solve problems. Look to the saints as models of people who used their gifts creatively in service to others. Help build the Kingdom of God as announced by Jesus.

This lesson will help you to:
- **explore** creative ways to express yourself.
- **appreciate** yourself as a person of integrity and virtue.
- **develop** ways to improve and use your abilities.

 What is one important quality you see in yourself that helps you to understand who you are?

Growing in Virtue

The virtue of **humility** leads to us acknowledge God as the Creator of all. This virtue strengthens us to be honest with ourselves and to accept ourselves and our relationship with God. A truly "humble" person is a person of integrity.

Being You in All Honesty

Many sixth-graders want to be somewhat like everyone else. They want to please others and to be accepted. While it is important for you to learn how to get along with others and to have friends, it is also very important for you to be honest with yourself and be the wonderful you God created you to be.

God calls you to get to know yourself honestly, to grow in that understanding, and to share the goodness of yourself with others. Knowing and accepting yourself, with all of your strengths and limitations, will give you an advantage in life. Knowing yourself can help you build self-confidence. Accepting yourself will strengthen you to face life with integrity and courage—and not give into the temptation to run yourself down.

You have a unique purpose, or vocation, in life. God calls you to know and accept that vocation. He has given it to you and is with you each day giving you the grace to know it and fulfill it. God desires for you to seek what is true, beautiful and good. So while you might face difficulties and challenges in life, you will have the strength in God's grace to deal with life's ups and downs. Saint Paul teaches us that God does not give us more than we can handle (see 1 Corinthians 10:13).

 Think about times when you had to be honest with yourself. How well did you do? Why?

Integrity

Integrity is the personal quality of being true to the person God created you to be. The virtue of humility strengthens you to be a person of integrity and to seek God and what is true, beautiful and good in the world.

The vocation God calls and invites you to freely accept is an important part of who you are. As you mature, you will more clearly discern God's vocation for you. It is like putting together a picture puzzle of who you are. There are various tools for learning about yourself. While psychologists and counselors certainly can help you discover certain aspects of your personality and how to relate to others in loving responsible ways, you must above all seek God's help.

God's help, his grace, comes to us through the Church. The sacraments, the reading of Sacred Scripture and prayer are sources of God's grace. The wisdom and teaching of the Church guide us in our search to know God and ourselves and to live according to his will.

Catholics Believe

One of the results of chaste living is achieving integrity of life and love. Chastity respects the unity of the whole person, body and soul.

"Self Discovery"

All of these tools can help you see that you are a person with dignity. Read below and act accordingly to discover the wonderful person God calls you to be.

Self-awareness. This means knowing and being conscious of your own personality and individuality. It means taking time to think about who you are, how you feel about things and what you've done.

Your own experience. Sometimes, when you've yearned for something such as a bicycle, you think that's the only thing that will ever make you happy. Yet you discover that the bicycle didn't really make you happy after all. Things aren't usually what make people happy. Look at your own experience and ask yourself, "What *does* make me happy?"

Honesty. When learning about yourself, it's important to be honest with yourself. You have to be brave enough to "own" everything about yourself, whether you like it or not. This means admitting your faults and mistakes as well as recognizing your talents and abilities.

Trust. If you trust yourself and others, you'll be able to say what you really think and to be who you really are. You'll be free to be yourself because you trust that you're a good person.

Freedom to choose. An important part of growing and learning is following the directions of other people who are older and wiser than you. But within that framework and within your own heart, you have many decisions to make. You can choose how you'll grow and change. You can begin now to follow your own dreams.

Perspective. Step back and look at some of the choices you've made. Ask yourself, "Why do I do the things I do?" Gradually you will be able to observe your own life a little more objectively, and this helps you understand who you are.

The experience of others. As you talk with your friends and family, you'll discover that you're a lot like them because you share many of the same dreams, struggles and fears. Another's experience may teach you how to avoid some mistakes or to keep trying when you want to give up.

All of these tools can help you see that you're a person with value and dignity, and that is a great discovery.

Catholic Family Album

Saint Hyacintha of Mariscotti

(1585–1640) was not always recognized as a Saint. In fact, through much of her life, the opposite was true. As a child Hyacintha was so unbearably self-centered, her parents sent her to live in a convent. While there she took vows to live as a nun, but for many years did not live out those vows. When she became seriously ill, Hyacintha took an honest look at her life and changed directions. With God's grace she became a model for younger nuns. She reached out to people in need and became well known not for being self-centered but for reaching out to elderly people who were poor. She was named a Saint of the Church in 1807.

Seeing the True Me

Sometimes it is easy to see the good things about yourself. And at other times, it is more difficult. Some days it is easier to see what you would like to change about yourself. And at other times, you may be less than honest with yourself.

When you prepare for the Sacrament of Penance and Reconciliation, you take the time to honestly examine your conscience. You take the time to ask the Holy Spirit to help you discern what you have done well and not so well, the right and wrong that you have done. You look honestly at how you need to change and grow to live as a disciple of Jesus Christ.

Use the chart below to take a good look at yourself. Ask the Holy Spirit to help you see yourself clearly. Remember, he knows you more than you know yourself. Briefly describe three of your best qualities or talents. Then, for each, write a plan of action. Include in your plan ways you will use that talent to help others. Be practical and specific in your planning.

TALENT	PLAN OF ACTION
1.	
2.	
3.	

Looking to the Future

Walk First

When Wilma Rudolph was sixteen years old, she made the United States Olympic track team. At twenty, she became the first female to win three gold medals in the same Olympic Games. Her skills were in track and field. Yet early in her life doctors had said she would never be able to walk.

When she was four years old, Wilma's left leg was paralyzed as the result of scarlet fever, a condition that was complicated by double pneumonia. Her mother refused to believe that Wilma would not walk. She took her daughter for weekly therapy treatments. She herself massaged Wilma's leg for hours each day; she taught Wilma's brothers and sisters how to massage her leg, too.

When she was eight, Wilma could walk with the aid of a brace. A year later, she began to wear a reinforced shoe. When she was eleven, Wilma threw away the shoe and, shortly after that, began playing basketball with her brothers. Wilma became a basketball star in high school and started running track.

In her first Olympic Games, Wilma was part of a relay team that won a bronze medal. Wilma's success certainly was due in part to talent. But she was able to use that talent fully because of desire, dedication and the faith of her family.

The life stories and achievements of many people tell of similar determination.

How do you relate to the dedication and determination of Wilma?

> **This lesson will help you to:**
> - **explore** the life story of a person with determination and dedication.
> - **understand** the importance of achieving goals.
> - **use** your imagination in setting and achieving goals.

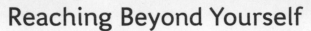

Growing in Virtue

The virtue of fortitude, or courage, is also one of the Seven Gifts of the Holy Spirit. It strengthens us for doing good. **Determination** takes courage of the heart, grounded with a sense of integrity, a capacity for resilience and an attitude of humility.

Reaching Beyond Yourself

Achieving any goal is like crossing the finish line. Some goals are easy to reach. Others are more difficult. Reaching goals requires determination, dedication, patience and perseverance. Having goals gives direction to your life. Goals help you focus on what you are doing and where you would like to head. Having clear, good goals can help you do your very best.

You must work hard to reach a goal you have set for yourself, as Wilma Rudolph did. You will not reach your goals immediately. For example, if you have set the goal of becoming a concert pianist, you will have to devote time toward learning the skills necessary for achieving your goal. You will have to practice, practice and practice.

Reaching your goals takes planning. You must think ahead and have a vision and "see the future." This vision will help you discipline yourself to work at achieving your goal. This vision will help you set priorities and make sacrifices.

You will have to put off certain other things that you would like to do now in order to reach your future goals. This means that you are willing to wait for the future reward. This is called delayed gratification. Instant gratification works the opposite. It means demanding and receiving your wants and desires immediately—right here, right now. Instant gratification is a dead end. It is a path leading to little or no personal growth. It prevents you from achieving future goals. Your success at achieving your long-term goals will be measured by your dedication and determination.

 Think about how well you deal with waiting for what you need or want.

Achieving the bigger goals in one's life often takes more time, discipline, planning or practice than it takes to achieve smaller goals. Working to achieve bigger goals require inner strength or determination. It requires using the Gifts of the Holy Spirit and the grace of God.

Determination has to do with three qualities of the heart: a sense of integrity, a capacity for resilience and an attitude of humility. Your integrity comes from your sense of self-worth. You gradually accept that your self-worth and that of others come from God.

Resilience is the courage to deal with failure, to bounce back and move ahead despite failure or difficulties. This kind of courage enables you to move past the temporary obstacles and focus on ways to improve for the future.

The virtue of humility allows you to accept yourself with all your God-given strengths and your limitations and to admit that you need the help of others. Everyone, at times, needs the assistance of someone who will listen and support their efforts.

Wilma Rudolph would never have achieved her Olympic goals without her dedication and determination and the support of her family and friends. You too can reach beyond yourself.

"Defining Success"

With a partner, write a definition of success in the space provided. Keep in mind integrity, resilience and humility. Share your definition with the class.

Catholics Believe

Jesus announced the Good News of the Kingdom of God. At Baptism, every Christian receives the mission, the responsibility and the grace to work toward the goal of the establishment of the kingdom.

Activity

Catholic Family Album

Matt Talbot (1846–1925) lived in Ireland. His family was very poor and Matt began working for a liquor company when he was only twelve years old to help his family. He began drinking very soon after he started working. It quickly became the most important thing in his life and he could not stop. When he was thirty years old, Matt set the goal to stop drinking and was determined to achieve it. He turned to God for help, began to go to Mass each day and often spent his free time praying to Mary. Matt achieved his goal and remained sober for the rest of his life. The Catholic Church has named Matt Talbot "Venerable." This is the first step in naming him a Saint of the Church.

Making My Dreams Come True

When Wilma Rudolph was twelve years old, she could not have known that she would be an Olympic champion. But she could have imagined how it would be to run with strength and grace. Wilma's dreams may also have included being a teacher or a mother or a coach, for she was all of these things after her competitive athletic career ended.

Your imagination lets you dream. Imagination is the ability to form a mental image of something that is not present or that does not exist. Your imagination helps you plan and dream about the future that may be yours someday. Your imagination is a gift from God—a gift that is a truly human power. Your imagination lets you "try on" different roles and ideas for yourself.

Consider for a moment that Wilma Rudolph's story might be found in a book entitled "Great Athletes of Our Time." Below complete the title of a book, in which your story might be told. Then imagine your future and write your story. Include two things you will do now to work toward that future.

Great _____ of Our Time

_____

_____

_____

_____

_____

Name ....

Summary

Remember what you have learned in each of the lessons in God's Gift of Self.

LESSON 3: Know Thyself

- God invites me to accept a vocation to use my gifts and talents in a loving and good way.
- I can discern the vocation God offers me by knowing myself and the talents and gifts he has given me.
- Integrity enables me to be the person God calls me to be.

LESSON 4: Looking to the Future

- Having goals gives direction to my life; achieving goals requires hard work, patience and perseverance.
- Determination takes courage of heart and is based on integrity, resilience and humility.
- God has given me the gift of imagination to help me plan and dream about my future.

Thinking It Through

1. How does humility help me know myself?

_____

_____

_____

2. How does a strong sense of my self-worth help me achieve my goals?

_____

_____

_____

3. How can the gift of creativity help me plan and attain my goals?

_____

_____

_____

Matching It Up

*On each line, write the letter of the description in Column B
that best goes with the term in Column A.*

 A

1. .... Humility

2. .... Integrity

3. .... Resilience

4. .... Imagination

5. .... Gifts of the Holy Spirit

 B

A. Human power that helps a person set long-term goals using their gifts and talents

B. The courage to deal with failure

C. Being true to the person you are

D. Being honest about yourself before God

E. God-given powers and strengths that enable us to work toward the establishment of the Kingdom of God

Name...

Recalling Key Concepts

Circle the T if the statement is true. Circle the F if the statement is false.

1. Once you make a goal, you cannot change it.   T   F
2. It is healthy to accept your strengths and your limitations.   T   F
3. The Church teaches that a sixth-grader is too young to bring goodness to others.   T   F
4. No two people think and respond exactly the same.   T   F
5. Achieving goals is simple, easy and quick.   T   F

Fill in the missing words in these sentences.

6. Studying before watching TV is an example of .... gratification.

7. Skipping practice to watch a movie is an example of .... gratification.

8. Knowing yourself can help build ....

9. .... was the first female to win three gold medals in the same Olympic Games.

10. Your .... lets you "try on" different ideas and dream about the future.

Working Together

Create a class booklet about people who have achieved their goals. Keep in mind the class' definition of success. Brainstorm as a class, a list of names. Include people from all walks of life, regardless of their notoriety or popularity. Working individually or in pairs, research and write a short article about one of the people named by the class. Use your creativity in doing this project.

God's Gift of Life

Sacrament of Family

The marriage between a baptized man and a baptized woman is a Sacrament, an outward sign of an inward grace given to the Church by Jesus. The marriage celebration is a reminder that the love between the couple is wonderful and holy. When a man and a woman promise to love each other forever in the Sacrament of Marriage, Jesus is there. The emotional and physical closeness they share helps them to follow Jesus more closely. The married couple become a sign of Christ's love for his Church.

Marriage calls a man and a woman to a life of self-giving love. One of the purposes of marriage is to have and to care for children. The other main purpose is to grow closer in love. These two purposes together bind people in a loving family.

In family life husband, wife and children share everything—happiness, sorrow, work, play and prayer. That is why the celebration of the Sacrament of Marriage is not only experienced in the ceremony but also in the day-to-day love of the family.

Family Blessings

Lord, give hope to those couples waiting to conceive or adopt a baby; give patience to parents who will soon give birth; and give courage to mothers alone and frightened during pregnancy. Help all families welcome every baby with joy and love. Amen.

Healthy Habits in the Home

Plan ways to celebrate in remembrance each family member's baptismal day. Think of that day as a second birthday, a spiritual birthday in which they were welcomed into the Church by Christ. Consider honoring this day with a prayer to the patron Saint of their name.

Taking the Lesson Home

Make a list of responsibilities for caring for a newborn.

List tasks and persons responsible, according to the baby's needs . . .

1. Feeding

2. Changing

3. Playing

4. Learning

5. Praying

Making Connections

Spend time with your child to talk about their birth and Baptism. Respond to these questions:

▶ How did you choose my name?

▶ How did you celebrate my arrival and Baptism?

▶ What was I like as a baby?

Faith on the Fridge

The family is at the heart of God's plan of creation. The Fourth Commandment teaches us that all members of a family are to honor and respect, love and care for one another.

Family Web Time
RCLBFamilyLife.com

Expecting a Baby

Hearing the Good News

Barbara Mitchell suspected that she might be pregnant. Her inclinations were strong, and she had been feeling a little nauseous in the mornings. A trip to the doctor confirmed the good news. When she and her husband, Kevin, announced the news to Rosie and Joe, their children, they danced around the room in excitement.

When Danielle and Michael Barella, who lived across the street, returned home one evening, they found a message on their answering machine. It was from Donna Wilson, their adoption counselor at Catholic Social Services. "Congratulations!" said Donna, "There is a newly born infant who is ready for you to adopt." Danielle and Michael were stunned. After five years of planning, their dream was finally coming true.

The two couples shared their good news with their families, close friends and co-workers. They began to think about what having a new baby would be like.

The Mitchells knew the importance of prenatal care. Barbara also knew that she and Kevin had to spend time preparing their children to welcome the new baby. The adoption agency had already counseled and tested the Barellas to determine their sense of responsibility to be parents.

Both families were experiencing many different emotions all at the same time—happiness, excitement, concern and love. Will the baby be a boy or a girl? What name will they choose? If the baby gets sick, will they know what to do? Will they have enough money to support the family? How can they be sure the child always feels loved?

Every day as they awaited the arrival of their new babies both families asked God for the wisdom and patience to love their child properly. They prayed that they would be good parents and could provide a loving home.

This lesson will help you to:

- **explore** and appreciate the concerns of parents who are expecting a baby.
- **understand** that the whole family is affected by a new member.
- **choose** one way that you will show that children are a blessing from God.

 What concerns might parents have today about having a baby?

A Time of Change

Two thousand years ago, in the small town of Bethlehem, Jesus was born into the loving family of Mary and Joseph. It was within this family that Jesus learned his first words and took his first steps. Mary and Joseph not only fed and clothed Jesus, they also taught him stories and prayers of God's Chosen People. They introduced him to God's Law. It was in the safe and loving home of the Holy Family that Jesus was born and grew up.

 Think about what it was like for Mary and Joseph to care for Jesus as a baby.

Families today experience the similar joys and struggles with caring for children as the Holy Family did. Babies are totally dependent on their parents' care for them. Parents not only provide food, clothing and shelter to a new baby; they also provide the baby with safety, love and a sense of belonging. They have responsibilities to help the baby grow physically, intellectually, emotionally and spiritually. The baby's life develops not only by being bundled in warm blankets but also by being wrapped in the love of a family.

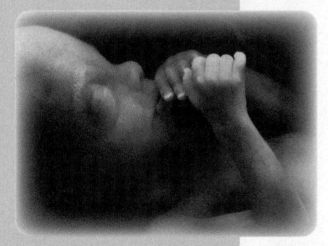

The development of a child in the womb of their mother is wonderful and complex. During a doctor's checkup, the parents can listen to the baby's heartbeat or see their baby in the womb using a sonogram. The mother can feel the baby moving and kicking inside her. The father, if he places his hand on his wife's abdomen, may also feel some sharp kicks.

Participating in God's creation of a new human being is a sacred act. To love and raise a child takes great energy and work for many years. That's why God wants the creation of new life to take place within the lifelong loving commitment of a marriage. The faithful love and unity of a husband and a wife is vital to ensure the healthy and holy upbringing of the baby.

During a pregnancy, each family member will experience a variety of emotions, including joy, sadness, frustration and excitement. All of these feelings are normal. Husband and wife do well to share their feelings with each other. This

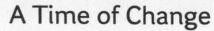

helps them to support each other during this exciting and wonderful time. Other children in the family may begin to think of how their lives may be changed with the addition of a brother or sister.

All family members can offer support and advice. This is a time when family members need to pull together and help out. It's a time of many wonderful changes.

Growing in Virtue

With **commitment** and **respect** members of a family can work together to create a home filled with peace and harmony, tenderness, forgiveness and self-giving love.

"Coping with Change"

On the chart provided, describe a recent change in your life and list what was good and not so good about it. Explain how you learned to cope with that change.

Activity

Change:

_____

_____

Good	Not So Good	Coping

Catholic Family Album

Project Gabriel is an outreach ministry supported by the Catholic Church. This ministry is named after Gabriel the Angel who announced the good news of life to Mary, helped dispel her anxiety and offered hope for the future. Project Gabriel lives out the Church's teaching that all human life from the moment of conception is to be valued and treated with dignity and respect. The people of Project Gabriel offer expectant mothers counseling and other support programs to guide the mother in honoring and protecting the life of her baby.

God's Blessing

The Old Testament shares with us the story of Hannah, a childless woman who prayed for a son. Read Hannah's story in 1 Samuel 1:1—2:21.

For all the worries and challenges that may come with being a parent, children are one of the greatest blessings God shares with married couples. The people of the Old Testament, as shown in the story of Hannah, valued children as a sign of God's blessing.

1. Summarize in your own words what the story of Hannah teaches about the gift of a child.

_____
_____
_____

2. Describe what society today does to show that they value or do not value children as a blessing and gift from God.

_____
_____
_____

3. What can and will you do to show that children (yourself included) are to be treated with respect and as a blessing and gift from God?

_____
_____
_____

A Baby Arrives

The Miracle of Birth

In the Mitchell and the Barella households, preparations were well underway for their new baby welcoming. The baby's bedroom had been wallpapered in one home, a crib repainted in the other and diapers bought in both. Each family had different circumstances, but both were equally excited about the arrival of their new baby.

One night, Barbara Mitchell awoke and shook her husband, Kevin. "This is it," she whispered. Kevin awoke instantly. "Okay," he said. "Let's get you to the hospital." On the way to the hospital, Kevin called their obstetrician, a doctor who is a specialist in pregnancy and childbirth, to inform him that the time had arrived and they were on their way to the hospital. Barbara had a very easy delivery. Her other children, Rosie and Joe, came to the hospital nursery that same afternoon to meet their new little sister.

In the Barella home, the big day arrived for Danielle and Michael, too. Donna Wilson called to share the wonderful news. It was time for them to come and meet their new baby and welcome him into their family. He was just three days old. When they arrived at the hospital, Donna met them and gave them the medical records of the baby's birth weight and length and the time of birth. As they held him for the first time, Danielle and Michael marveled at the miracle of new life in their arms.

Both families were excited about the arrival of their new baby. The hospital's pediatrician, or children's doctor, reassured each couple that their baby was healthy and ready to go home.

Though babies are born every day, each new birth is always mysterious and wondrous. Children are truly a great blessing from God.

This lesson will help you to:

- **explore** and appreciate welcoming a baby into a family.
- **understand** the importance of caring for a newborn.
- **claim** your identity as a child of God.

What experiences have you had of welcoming a new baby into a family?

Life with a New Baby

Even when parents have prepared well, giving care to an infant changes a family's life. A baby stirs up a swirl of activity: feeding, changing diapers, bathing and doing laundry. Babies can cry, kick, wave their fists and look around, but babies cannot survive without the help of their family. Newly born infants depend on family members to feed them, dress them, talk to them, provide a safe place for them to sleep, keep them clean and pray for them.

Caring for a baby is a way of communicating with the baby. When a parent feeds a baby, the baby learns how the mother or the father looks, smells, sounds and smiles. The baby feels warm, cared for and loved. When the baby is bathed or changed, they can tell if this is being done gently and lovingly or impatiently. The baby can tell if the words being spoken are kind and loving or angry. Even at this early stage, a baby can already recognize the faces, touches and voices of the family.

 Think about some of the things you can do to care for a newborn.

Caring for a New Baby

A baby requires more than just feeding and changing. The parents, brothers and sisters and grandparents all need to talk to, cuddle, play with and sing to the baby. The baby needs to be rocked, to see smiles and to hear lots of laughter. All of these loving and caring interactions between baby and parent, as well as between baby and other family members, do much more than give the baby exercise and attention. They help the baby learn to love and to play. They help the baby to relate to others.

Families who surround their baby with love are strong, happy and holy. Babies learn to love when their parents and other family members express their love through words, actions, gestures and spirit. Babies, in other words, grow in love and learn to love by being loved.

"Baby Needs"

Think about the many needs of a baby. List four of those needs in the space provided. Explain how each of these needs of a baby can be met.

Need of the Newborn	Meeting the Need
1.	
2.	
3.	
4.	

Catholic Family Album

Catholics honor certain Saints as patron Saints. The devotion of Catholics to patron Saints flows from the fact that the Church is a Communion of Saints, the faithful living on earth and those who have died. Catholics believe that we can communicate with the members of the Church in Heaven and trust in their love for us and desire to help us. **Margaret of Antioch** is a Saint who lived during the Middle Ages. She was killed because of her faith. Today Margaret is honored as the patron Saint of childbirth.

Claiming My Identity

What do you remember about your Baptism? Here are a few important things to remember.

In the Sacrament of Baptism, a person is reborn of water and the Holy Spirit. The baptized person is made a sharer in the very life of God and becomes an adopted son or daughter of God. Here are some other things that happen at Baptism:

- Baptism joins a person to Jesus Christ and the baptized person is welcomed as a member of the Church, the Body of Christ.
- A baptized person receives the gift of the Holy Spirit and the grace necessary to live as a faithful follower of Jesus.
- Baptism forgives Original Sin and all personal sins. A new member gets a fresh start.
- Baptism unites a person with all the baptized, living and dead. Every baptized person receives forever the mark or the identity of being a Christian with all the rights and responsibilities of being a Christian.

In this space design your own Christian identity badge. Include words or symbols that explain who you are and the things you will do to live as a follower of Jesus.

Name ....

Summary

Remember what you have learned in each of the lessons in God's Gift of Life.

LESSON 5: Expecting a Baby

- God wants the creation of new life to take place within the loving commitment of marriage.
- A child is a person and a blessing from God from the first moment of conception.
- Families experience joy and accept the responsibility to care for their children.

LESSON 6: A Baby Arrives

- The birth of every baby is a sign of the great mystery of God's love.
- Caring for a baby communicates love to the baby and a sense of belonging.
- In Baptism a person is made a sharer in new life in Christ and is marked with the identity of being a Christian forever.

Thinking It Through

1. Why do parents need to be mature and responsible?

   _____

   _____

   _____

2. What are some ways you can show your love for a newborn?

   _____

   _____

   _____

3. How can family members help each other appreciate and live their baptismal promises?

   _____

   _____

   _____

Matching It Up

On each line, write the letter of the description in Column B that best goes with the term in Column A.

 A

 B

1. .... Respect

2. .... Family

3. .... Pregnancy

4. .... Abortion

5. .... Baptism

A. Nine-month period of development in the womb

B. Ending the life of an unborn child

C. Virtue that helps families create a home filled with peace and harmony, tenderness, forgiveness and self-giving love

D. Sacrament in which a person is made a sharer in new life in Christ

E. School of virtue

Name ....

Recalling Key Concepts

Circle the T if the statement is true. Circle the F if the statement is false.

1. A baby can recognize familiar touches and voices of family members.   T   F

2. A baby's senses are underdeveloped and do not need stimulation.   T   F

3. The Church supports families in their efforts to adopt a child.   T   F

4. If a pregnant woman is healthy, she does not need prenatal care.   T   F

5. The Church welcomes children into its family through Baptism.   T   F

Fill in the missing words in these sentences.

6. Babies are totally dependent on their .... to care for them.

7. The .... gives new life in Christ, forgives sins and welcomes the person into the Church.

8. Participating in God's creation of a new human being is a

    .... act.

9. .... are a blessing from God.

10. Human life begins at the moment of ....

Working Together

Find out when the celebration of the Sacrament of Baptism will take place in your parish. Plan on attending the celebration as a family. Prepare for the event by making individual welcome cards for the newly baptized. On each card, say how the parish is a good place for the new member to grow as a Catholic. Offer your prayers and good works for the one to be baptized.

You Are My Friends

In the Gospels we see that Jesus loved people who were definitely not part of the "in crowd." Story after story tells about Jesus' love for all people. Jesus loves the blind and the lame, the sick and healthy, the poor and the rich, men and women and children. He loved people who others considered to be holy and those judged to be sinners. Jesus took time to listen to them to teach them and to heal them. For example, at dinner in the home of a prominent Pharisee, Jesus showed respect and mercy for a woman who crashed the party. Despite the protests of the host, Jesus forgave the woman's sins because of her great love (read Luke 7:36–50).

Jesus called his followers "friends." He taught them to respect others and showed how to translate that respect into action. Being a friend of Jesus means sharing what you have, welcoming newcomers, seeing others as children of God and showing respect for everyone. Through the teachings and example of Jesus, we learn what God wants of us, his followers. Recognize today how you can love others as Jesus loves you.

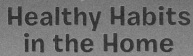

Healthy Habits in the Home

As you arrange family chores and remind others of family rules, be sure to explain how doing these family chores and living by family rules shows respect not only for each family member, but also for guests who you invite into your home and to God who is always present with your family.

Family Blessings

Lord, we ask you to heal our family and friends who are sick in body and in spirit. Comfort them in their time of need, letting them know they are in our thoughts and prayers. Amen.

Taking the Lesson Home

Make a list of ways the family can show respect to those in the family, parish or community according to their needs.

List respectful ways of responding to the needs of others for:

1. Clothing
2. Health care
3. Entertainment
4. Education
5. Prayer

Making Connections

Discuss as a family the topic of aging and dying. Have each member of the family share their responses to these questions:

▸ Who in our family is happily growing old? Who is having difficulties?

▸ How have we dealt with the death of someone close?

▸ What questions do you have about the Church's attitude toward death and her teachings on respect for life?

Faith on the Fridge

All praise be yours, my Lord,
through those who endure sickness and trial.
Happy are those who wait in peace,
for you will reward them.
And all praise be yours, my God,
even in shining Sister Death,
  who comes to us all.
Happy are those she finds doing your will,
for no lasting death can touch them!
(Prayer by Saint Francis of Assisi)

Family
Web Time
RCLBFamilyLife.com

Respect Thyself

Signs of Respect

"Let's go skateboarding tomorrow," suggested Roger, as he joined his friends in the back of the school bus one Friday afternoon. "Yeah, sure," Jeff said. "No," Terry protested, "That means Michael can't go." Jeff complained, "Ah, he can't do anything!" Roger urged, "OK, let's think of something else." Tim shouted, "I know! How about the wildlife preserve? It has a special nature trail for wheelchairs." They all agreed.

"Hey, guys," interrupted Susan from three seats up, where she was sitting with Ella and Gloria. "Sounds like fun. Can we come, too?" The answers were varied: "Get lost . . . It's a free world . . . Sure, the more the merrier."

The following afternoon, the boys gathered at the wildlife preserve. There was a big sign stating the trail rules: No food or drinks. No pets. No radios. No skateboards. While they waited for the girls to arrive, two of the boys picked up some soda cans that were lying around and put them into a recycle bin.

Everyone was in high spirits as the group started the hike. Suddenly, a big dog came running down the trail. Ella started screaming, "Get away from me!" Some of the boys laughed. "It's only a dog," Tim sneered. "There aren't supposed to be any dogs here," Gloria spoke up, "I'm going to tell the ranger when we get back."

The group stopped to admire the variety of birds gathered at the lake's edge. They laughed at the antics of a squirrel as it scurried up and over the rocks. "We'd better get going," said Terry. "My sister will be here to pick us up soon. I don't want to keep her waiting." They rounded the last loop and headed for the end of the trail.

> This lesson will help you to:
> - **explore** why respect is a way of honoring a person.
> - **discover** how self-respect affects a person's choices.
> - **commit** to following rules as a sign of respect.

 Which activity would you have chosen for your group of friends? Why?

Taking Another Look

The word *respect* comes from a Latin word meaning "to look at again." When you respect someone, you "take another look." You don't allow first impressions to determine how you think about someone. Instead, you look a bit closer and deeper to see the real person.

Showing respect for a person is based on three attitudes: empathy, altruism and moral awareness. Empathy is sensitivity to the needs and feelings of others. Altruism is the willingness to put the needs of others before your own. When you consider how your actions will affect others, you demonstrate moral awareness. When you show respect for other people, they tend to treat you with respect in return. In addition, you feel good about your dealings with others. You show respect for yourself too.

 Think about some of the ways you show respect toward others and yourself.

Imagine that you are walking home from school and you see some older students teasing, pushing and taunting a younger person. You step in and protect this younger kid, taking the time to walk him home safely, encouraging him and reminding him that those kids are just bullies. As you begin heading back home, you see a bird that has apparently been wounded lying on the ground. You grab a box out of a nearby garbage can and rescue the bird. Finally, when you arrive home, you see your older brother's friends hanging out front. They are smoking cigarettes and tell you that you should have one too. You feel tempted because you want them to like you, but you choose to smile and say, "No thanks." You head inside for a snack.

You might have a huge range of emotions and thoughts as you walked home. Yet, in the end, you would likely not only feel "good" after each event, but you would probably also feel "real good" about yourself. Because when you act in a loving and compassionate way, you are actually respecting the deepest part of yourself. Deep in your heart, you will find the truest image of yourself, your likeness to God.

Expressing who you are on the outside can be a good way of showing respect for yourself and to others. How you express that respect should reflect the image of your true self.

God created you, as a unique expression of his artwork, like a beautiful church (see I Corinthians 6:19, Ephesians 2:10). The practice of holding onto and guarding the sacred image of yourself is called modesty. Modesty is a virtue that frees you to be an image of God. You show modesty in the way you talk, dress and act. The Church reminds us through her teachings that practicing modesty can help us to be respectful of ourselves and to grow in self-confidence.

Growing in Virtue

Modesty protects the intimate center of the person. It is rooted in an intuition of the spiritual dignity of the person. Teaching modesty means awakening in people respect for the human person.

"Tough Choices"

In the space provided list four tough choices that you might have to make. Also include how you would handle each tough choice.

Tough Choice	I would handle it by . . .

Catholic Family Album

Saint Martin of Tours was born to a wealthy noble family in the 4th century. He lived his faith in word and deed, in ways that showed respect for others and for himself. One day he encountered a beggar while traveling. He cut his cloak in half and gave half to the beggar. Later Martin had a vision of Christ wearing part of his cloak. At the age of fifteen, he had joined the Roman imperial army, but later refused to engage in combat on moral principle and religious beliefs. He was dismissed and became a student under Saint Hilary of Poitiers. Eventually, Martin became the bishop of Tours, France and lived the life of a hermit.

Respect Is the Rule

You are expected to follow many rules: family rules, school rules, playground rules, game rules, rules of good manners. Following good rules is a good way to show respect both for yourself and others. One of the most basic rules is the Golden Rule (see Matthew 7:12). It applies at all times and in any place.

Look at the following rules. Explain how following each shows respect for yourself and for others. Then add two more rules that you are expected to follow and tell how they help you show respect.

1. During a test, keep your eyes on your own paper.
   _____

2. Call home if you are going to be late.
   _____

3. Do not laugh when someone makes a mistake or has an accident.
   _____

4. _____
   _____

5. _____
   _____

Aging and Death

The Weaver

The elderly Navajo woman sat at her loom. Her keen, black eyes swept over the rug that she was weaving. It was almost finished. She thought about all that had gone into this rug: raising and shearing the sheep, washing the wool, preparing the wool for spinning and dying the yarn.

"Yes, that and much more," she thought, "But now, well, I can still sit at my loom and weave." She brushed back a strand of silver hair that had escaped from the heavy coil on the back of her head. Her daughters said that her designs improved with age. No two were ever exactly the same. "They certainly are in demand, no denying that," she mused. All the while, her fingers continued to work, nimbly and expertly. After so many years of weaving, they knew exactly what to do.

A slow smile spread across her wrinkled face when she thought of all her children, grandchildren and great grandchildren to whom she passed on her weaving skills. She had also taught the family patterns and colors. "All in all," she thought, "It has been a good life. I am satisfied."

The elderly woman accepted the fact that she could not do all of the things that she had once done. She depended on the younger ones to do many of those things for her now, just as they had depended on her when they were young. But she knew that they still needed her. They came to her when they wanted to talk. She knew how to listen. Her calmness and quietness was reassuring to them. She was proud of her work but more proud of her children. She had overcome many struggles and learned how to love her way through life. Someday ahead, the woman knew she would weave her last rug.

This lesson will help you to:

- **explore** the joys and struggles of aging.
- **respect** elderly people as contributors of wisdom and insight.
- **understand** the Christian attitude toward death.

 What wisdom or skill have you learned from your grandparents or someone older?

A Matter of Respect

You may feel, as you enter puberty, as though you have been launched into a whole different universe. The same thing happens again for people who age as seniors. Elderly people must learn to deal with changes in their work life, relationships, finances and health. Retiring from a long career is a new situation that can challenge a person's self-esteem. The loss of a spouse, the difficulties of living on a fixed income, chronic or terminal illness are other common challenges faced by elderly people.

But aging is not all pain and struggle, just as adolescence is not all awkwardness and confusion. Many elderly people find new interests and energy. They enjoy past and new hobbies, spend time with family members, take classes, continue or begin volunteer work and sometimes travel. Seniors joyfully share their wisdom and memories, but they also enjoy having the time to create new memories.

Think about some of the challenges that accompany old age.

Enjoying the gifts of aging and facing its challenges, especially the reality of death, might be easier if society had a healthier attitude toward the aging process. Many people, elderly and young, do not want to be reminded of the pain and loss associated with suffering and dying. Much of society tries to control disease and prevent death; not enough effort is put into helping people face these human experiences with courage and grace.

The Catholic Church has a much more positive approach toward aging and dying than much of society. The Church's teachings and actions promote respecting and valuing elderly people even in times of their suffering and dying. People are worthy of respect no matter what their age or condition of health. Aging and death are part of the natural cycle of life. Physical death is the doorway to eternal life.

When you show elderly people the respect they deserve (the respect they have a right to), you will learn a lot about how to love life at any stage. The stories and insights of elderly people can teach you how to enjoy your life and to face everyday problems with patience, endurance and a sense of humor.

Through the sharing of the experiences of the elderly, you can grow in wisdom. Wisdom is the gift of the Holy Spirit that empowers us to see and value life as God sees and values every human person. The practice of propriety guides us in being truly respectful in speech and conduct, not only to the elderly but to all people. Self-respect is learned over time and refines a person. It enables one to better appreciate oneself as a child of God. Like the Navajo weaver did for her family, elderly people can help you gain respect for yourself and for others.

Growing in Virtue

The practice of **propriety** guides us in choosing to do and say things that express respect for others and for ourselves in appropriate ways. Good manners flow from propriety, a reflection of prudence. Good manners demonstrate the proper respect and honor due to people at every stage of life.

"Best at Every Stage of Life"

For each category below, write one or two things you have done and can do now so that you are at your best at every stage of life.

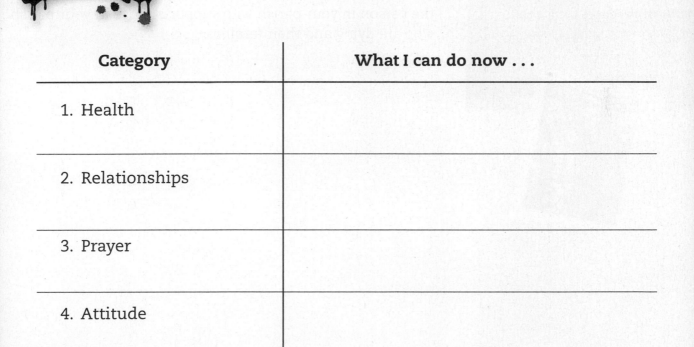

Activity

Category	What I can do now . . .
1. Health	
2. Relationships	
3. Prayer	
4. Attitude	

Catholic Family Album

Saint Anthony of Padua

(1195–1231) was a Franciscan Friar who became a great preacher and is honored by the Catholic Church with the title Doctor of the Church. While he traveled and preached through Europe, Saint Anthony spent much of his time in the Italian town of Padua. While in Padua, Anthony became known for reconciling differences, healing the affirmed and respecting the dignity of every person. The Catholic Church celebrates the life and work of Saint Anthony of Padua on June 13.

Sharing My Faith in Life Everlasting

Death can be a frightening word. Thinking about dying can be strange and discomforting at times. As Catholics we know that we will die. We believe that death is not an end; it is a new beginning because Jesus overcame death. On the third day, he rose again to a new and glorified life. The Resurrection of Jesus shows us that death is not the end. Death is only the beginning of new life with God, a life that is everlasting.

One way Catholics help people who are terminally ill and their family is by providing hospice care. In a hospice, people receive physical and spiritual care in their home or in another home-like setting, not in a hospital. Hospice care shows respect for the person and provides the support they need while they deal with their dying.

Read the story of Lazarus in the Gospel of John 11:1–3, 17–44. In the space below design a message card about death. Your card should show both sorrow over loss and hope in life forever with God. Include in your design, Jesus' words, "I am the resurrection and the life" (John 11:25). Give your card to the person in your parish who supports those in your parish who are dying and their families.

Name ....

Summary

Remember what you have learned in each of the lessons in God's Gift of Love.

LESSON 7: Respect Thyself

- Respect is an attitude that recognizes the sacredness of every human person.
- Self-respect lets you recognize your own sacredness, calling you to make good choices.
- A modest person recognizes the sacredness of the body, guarding themselves as a treasure and seeing others in the same way.

LESSON 8: Aging and Death

- Aging involves changes in every aspect of living, resulting in the joys and struggles of life.
- Good manners follow from an attitude of respect and enable one to shine as a child of God.
- Death is a natural part of life and a passageway to eternal life.

Thinking It Through

1. Explain how self-respect is the basis of all respect.

   _____

   _____

   _____

2. How is showing respect for self and others a way to show God respect?

   _____

   _____

   _____

3. What can help you to have a more realistic and accepting attitude toward aging and death?

   _____

   _____

   _____

Matching It Up

On each line, write the letter of the description in Column B that best goes with the term in Column A.

 A

1. .... Altruism

2. .... Death

3. .... Empathy

4. .... Eternal Life

5. .... Respect

B

A. Recognizing the sacredness in every person

B. The promise to those who follow Jesus

C. A natural passage to everlasting life

D. Willingness to put the needs of others before your own

E. Sensitivity to the needs and feelings of others

Name...

Recalling Key Concepts

Circle the T if the statement is true. Circle the F if the statement is false.

1.	The Church has the same view of death as most of society.	T	F
2.	The Golden Rule says to love God and others.	T	F
3.	Eating nutritiously is a way of showing self-respect.	T	F
4.	Self-respect shows up in the way you act, dress and talk.	T	F
5.	As we age, we become less valuable to society and to our families.	T	F

Fill in the missing words in these sentences.

6. A .... person recognizes the sacredness of the body by guarding themselves as a treasure and seeing others in the same way.

7. The good manners that follow from .... demonstrate the proper respect and honor due to people at every stage of life.

8. When you consider how your actions will affect others, you

demonstrate ....

9. Jesus' .... shows that physical death is the doorway

to ....

10. People are worthy of respect no matter what their age or

condition of ....

Working Together

With a partner or as a class, find a way to become involved on a regular basis with elderly people. You might join your parish ministry that cares for the elderly or visit the homebound or terminally ill. You could become pen pals with people at the local senior citizens' center. Hold each other accountable to this commitment.

Works of Mercy

Mercy is one of the qualities that deepens relationships best between individuals, families and nations. Another way of describing mercy is loving-kindness or compassion, which flows from the mercy God bestows on us. Over the centuries, Christians took the words of Jesus in the parable of the Judgment of Nations in Matthew 25:31–46 and made them into a list of actions called the Corporal Works of Mercy. They are:

- Feed the hungry.
- Give drink to the thirsty.
- Give clothes to those who have none.
- Shelter the homeless.
- Visit the sick.
- Visit the imprisoned.
- Bury the dead.

Catholics have traditionally valued each of these works. Participating in groups that do such good works is an excellent way for families to fulfill their responsibility to care for others, especially people in need.

Healthy Habits in the Home

As a family activity, compile a household inventory of what the family owns. List the items according to the categories "Belonging to the Whole Family" or "Belonging to *Specific Name*." Evaluate how each item contributes to the good of the family and shows how wisely the family chooses to spend its money.

Family Blessings

Lord, move us to be generous with all that you have provided us. Teach us to continue to use all that we have to honor you by helping people in need. Amen.

Taking the Lesson Home

Discuss as a family this list of ways a family might live the Golden Rule, which expands upon the concepts learned in this unit.

List ways in which the family lives out the Golden Rule while:

1. Sharing a meal together

2. Traveling to visit a family

3. Shopping with a friend or relative

4. Teaching how to do or learn something

5. Worshiping at Mass

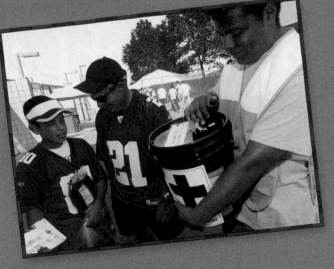

Making Connections

Discuss the topic of stewardship. Have each member of the family respond to the following questions:

▶ How do I help meet the needs of our family?

▶ How can we as a family share our material and spiritual blessings with others?

▶ What difficulties do I have in spending money wisely?

▶ How can we as a family do more to support the Church?

Faith on the Fridge

O Lady of Good Remedy, source of unfailing help, grant that we may draw from your treasury of graces in our time of need. Touch the hearts of sinners, that they may seek reconciliation and forgiveness. Bring comfort to the afflicted and the lonely; help the poor and the hopeless; aid the sick and the suffering. May they be healed in body and strengthened in spirit to endure their sufferings with patient resignation and Christian fortitude. Amen.

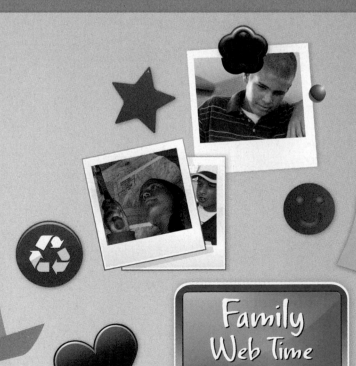

Family
Web Time
RCLBFamilyLife.com

It All Adds Up

Judy Dunne is the director of the diocesan center that provides services for the unemployed and the homeless. She is responsible for taking care of the money the center receives. Every year she prepares a financial report for the center detailing how the money is being used to support its work.

In the report, all the money the center spends to provide services is called expenses. All the money the center receives is called income. Most of the income includes donations from a variety of people and organizations. Part of the report also includes a budget, which lists expected expenses and anticipated income.

When Judy added up the numbers this year, she noticed that fewer people came to the center for help than the previous year. That was good news. Judy knew that this was a sign that the local economy was improving and more people were working. The economy refers to the way in which the resources of a country or a community are managed. Therefore, economics refers to the science or study of dealing with money. Judy also knew that there were still many families struggling with poverty, joblessness and homelessness.

The service center of the diocese does not try to make a profit. A profit is the amount of money left over after all the expenses have been subtracted from the income. The service center operates as an extension of the Church's mission to help those in need and thus is non-profit in monetary terms.

As Judy always says, "Our profit is the joy of helping others."

This lesson will help you to:

- **explore** the use of money in society.
- **understand** the importance of fiscal responsibility.
- **identify** ways to discern the proper use of money.

What are some non-profit organizations like this diocesan center that you might consider helping?

Catholics Believe

Economic activity and its systems are to provide for the needs of people. A system that subordinates a person to production or profit violates their dignity and rights. Work is for the person, not the person for work.

Family Finances

Every family has the responsibility to be good and wise stewards of the family's income. This responsibility is called fiscal responsibility. They are to use their income to support the well-being of their family. Families also have the responsibility to share with others who are unable to fulfill their own need for food, housing and other basic needs.

The family budget is a tool to make sure that money is being managed wisely and well. The family budget can be a few lines on the back of an envelope, a simple spreadsheet on the computer or a complex software program that tracks finances and generates budget reports. A budget helps parents plan for the future and to make sure that there is money for savings, for emergencies and for sharing with people in need.

To make a budget, a family first estimates its yearly income. Then the family estimates expenses. When the expenses are subtracted from the income, the money that is left over can be put into savings or can be set aside for emergencies. If the expenses are greater than the income, the family might fall into debt. If debt gets too great, a family can be in serious financial trouble.

Worrying about money is one of the greatest causes of stress in a family. Parents want to provide for their children. But sometimes loss of a job, unforeseen medical expenses and buying of "extras" can get in the way of having the money to provide for the basic needs of the family. You can help your family to stay within its budget. You can help your family by learning to use money wisely yourself.

 Think about how you spend and save money.

Some people think that all their problems would be solved if they could only hit the jackpot or win the lottery. Some people are driven by their desire for more and more. Such a desire can become the root cause of many other problems. This desire is called greed. It blinds us to the blessings we have and traps us in a lifestyle that never satisfies us and can harm a family in many ways.

The Catholic Church teaches that money can be considered part of God's gifts. Yet it is not a sign by which we judge our favor with God. It is one way by which a person's work is justly compensated. The Church teaches that our response to money can be summarized in two words: gratitude and generosity. We are to thank God for all that he has provided and be willing to share what we have with others.

A family lives the virtues of gratitude and generosity by including tithing and almsgiving in its normal budget. Tithing is giving money in support of the Church on a regular basis. Almsgiving is sharing our blessings with people in need. This kind of stewardship builds respect for oneself and for others.

Growing in Virtue

Stewardship in the form of fiscal responsibility shows honor for the gifts and resources provided by God. The use of money is a means to an end, which is to provide for the needs of the individual, families and society.

"Value of Money"

In the space provided, or on a separate sheet of paper, design a bumper sticker that tells the value of money. Do not be afraid to make your sticker humorous.

Activity

Setting Rules of Thumb

Sometimes having a couple of rules committed to memory is helpful in being able to act in a moral way. These "rules of thumb" (as they are called) can help you make good and wise decisions to practice fiscal responsibility.

Here are a few rules of thumb for the wise use of money:

- Needs of people come first.
- Don't waste money on foolish things.
- Use of money should make you a better person.
- Take care of your possessions.
- Be charitable with your money.

Setting these rules of thumb and learning to live by them now will help you grow as person who is fiscally responsible.

Read each of the following cases, keeping the rules of thumb in mind. After each case, write the rule of thumb that was used or was not used. Then select a rule of thumb you have or can practice and how you do or can live by it.

1. The movie was fantastic. Tim loved it so much he went out and bought the video game based on the movie. One of his friends told him the game was a dud, so Tim never tried it. It is still unopened.

_____

2. Mark really needed a bike to get to school. He was saving money he got for extra chores around the farm, sweeping the chicken coop and gathering eggs. One day, he blew his savings on three downloads and a hot fudge sundae.

_____

3. My rule of thumb:

_____

I will live it by

_____ .

Worldwide Family

See with God's Eyes

Every two years, the Olympics Games occur. From around the world, hundreds of athletes come together to compete. Watching the games can give you a sense of many different cultures and traditions.

People in every nation of the world can watch the Olympics because of technology. The whole world is connected by technology. We are hardly ever out of touch with the rest of the world. At any time, you can turn on a television, log onto the Internet, call a relative or text a friend. Today you can be "live and online" with the world.

For the Christian, global communication reinforces our understanding of one of the most basic truths of the Catholic Church: all men and women are brothers and sisters in the Family of God. We are connected by our human nature and our desire to love and serve the Lord. Yet we are also connected by our brokenness through sin.

Many of the events around the world are unhappy and tragic. People do not always treat one another like brothers and sisters. Daily we hear of and even witness examples of crime, violence, prejudice, hate, war, famine, oppression and terrorism.

Yet when we see with God's eyes, we not only recognize the injustice in the world that results from sin, but also the hope found in living our Catholic faith. This hope lies in the reality that God's promises will come true. God's kingdom of justice, peace and love is coming about and will be fulfilled when Christ comes again in glory.

Blessed Pope John XXIII saw the world with God's eyes. In his encyclical letter, *Peace on Earth,* Pope John XXIII listed the rights of every person, which are the common needs of all people. We are called to protect these fundamental rights and to preserve them as we prepare for the coming of our Savior, Jesus Christ, and his kingdom.

This lesson will help you to:

- **explore** that all people are your spiritual brothers and sisters.
- **understand** the importance of caring for our neighbors.
- **choose** to act in accord with the Golden Rule.

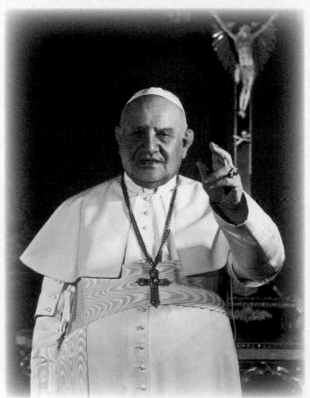

 What ways do you feel connected to others who live in a different part of the world?

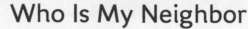

Catholics Believe

The common good considers the needs of every individual. Prudence is necessary in order to achieve such justice. We are animated by love in seeking the good of all. We can work together to prepare the way for the coming of the Kingdom of God.

Who Is My Neighbor

When Jesus was asked what it means to be a part of God's kingdom, he responded, "Love God with your whole heart and soul, and love your neighbor as yourself" (based on Luke 10:27).

Someone in the crowd attempted to trick Jesus. "Who is my neighbor?" he asked. Jesus answered, as he so often did, with a story. The story was the parable of the Good Samaritan. (Read Luke 10:29–37.) After he told the parable, Jesus asked the man who questioned him, "Who was neighbor to that man?" The man answered, "The one who treated him with mercy" (Luke 10:37).

 Think about which person from the parable you are most like.

Being a neighbor means walking in the shoes of others. It means understanding and accepting the reality that we belong to the same family, the Family of God. How do we show this? Jesus taught that we are to feed the hungry, give drink to the thirsty, help strangers, give clothes to those who need them, help the sick and visit the imprisoned (see Matthew 25:35–39). The Church names these actions the Corporal Works of Mercy.

Being aware of people who are in need is the first step in reaching out to help them. Before you can put these acts of mercy into action, you must see people with those needs. That kind of awareness means really looking at people who sometimes are "invisible." Such people might include the poor, the elderly and those who are lonely. So be attentive to others and their needs.

God expects people to respect one another and to support each other in meeting their basic needs. For example, everyone needs and deserves to live a healthy and safe life. Living the Ten Commandments and the Beatitudes are universal ways in which we can do that. With our imagination and intellect, we can find ways to follow Jesus who said, "Whatever you did for one of these least brothers [and sisters] of mine, you did for me" (Matthew 25:40).

We are called to use the resources God has provided to work for the good of all people, the common good. God gives us the vision and grace to use our resources in creative ways. No family can do everything alone, but each family can contribute to the betterment of society. Each of us can reach out and care for somebody in need, using our gifts from God for the common good. This is at the heart of using our ingenuity.

Growing in Virtue

As we seek to help one another and work for the common good, the diversity of peoples and their gifts can lead to creative ways of promoting the common good. The gift of **ingenuity** helps us achieve that goal. We can unite all our gifts and work together toward justice and peace.

"Creative Mercy"

Imagine that a person has chosen not to live by one of the Commandments or Beatitudes listed below or by another one of your choosing. How might you respond with merciful kindness to help that person to do better?

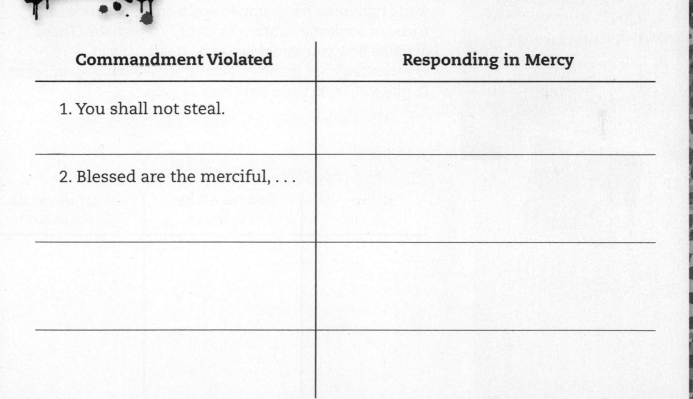

Activity

Commandment Violated	Responding in Mercy
1. You shall not steal.	
2. Blessed are the merciful, . . .	

Catholic Family Album

The life and work of **Saint John of Matha** (1160–1213) provides us an example of a person who worked for every person's basic right to freedom. John founded a group who worked to free Christian slaves. They prayed to Mary to guide them in their work. They raised money to purchase the slaves so they could give them their freedom. They were so successful that John honored Mary with the title Our Lady of the Good Remedy. Many in Europe and Latin America today give devotion to Mary using this title during times of need.

Living by the Golden Rule

In the Gospel of Matthew, Jesus taught his disciples that they were to live by the Golden Rule; namely, they were to treat others the way they want to be treated (see Matthew 7:12). The Golden Rule, just as the Commandments and Beatitudes, guides us to work for the good and well-being of others. It reminds us all that we belong to a worldwide community.

The people of the world differ in language, religion and many other ways. Perhaps too often we focus on those differences as things that divide us. Those differences are also too often the cause of fear and misunderstanding, which can lead to prejudice.

But these differences make the world a fascinating place. They can make known the beauty of God's plan of Creation. If we value each other as God values us, as brothers and sisters belonging to the Family of God, our diversity will unite us instead of divide us.

On the chart, list a problem affecting people around the world right now, for example, world hunger. Work with a friend or someone at home to identify a problem. Then, describe how you would like to be treated if you were experiencing that problem. Finally, state what you and your family will begin to do right now to help.

THE GOLDEN RULE

Global Problem	How I would like to be treated	What we can do to help

Name ....

Summary

Remember what you have learned in each of the lessons in God's Gift of Community.

LESSON 9: Family Economics

- Christian families are called to use their money wisely. Developing and using a budget helps a family manage their money wisely.
- The Catholic Church teaches that a society whose economic system subordinates a person to production or profits violates the person's dignity.
- Stewardship in the form of fiscal responsibility shows gratitude to God for the gifts and resources he provides for us.

LESSON 10: Worldwide Family

- All people are brothers and sisters in the Family of God.
- The common good is the total of all things that people need to reach their God-given potential and to live with dignity.
- Each of us is responsible to support one another in working for the common good.

Thinking It Through

1. Why are some people more likely to live in poverty than others?

   _____

   _____

   _____

2. How can the stereotypes we have of people blind us to their needs?

   _____

   _____

   _____

3. What does honesty have to do with fiscal responsibility?

   _____

   _____

   _____

   _____

Matching It Up

On each line, write the letter of the description in Column B that best goes with the term in Column A.

A   **B**

1. .... Budget

2. .... Common Good

3. .... Ingenuity

4. .... Wisdom

5. .... Stewardship

A. The Gift of the Holy Spirit that enables us to see and value people and all of creation as God does

B. Skills that are creative or clever for the benefit of others

C. The actions of caring for what God has given us in service to others

D. A financial tool to aid in managing money

E. The sum total needs of a given community to live

Name...

Recalling Key Concepts

Circle the T if the statement is true. Circle the F if the statement is false.

1. Jesus said that we would be judged by the way we treat others.   T   F
2. Tithing is giving the majority of our money to others.   T   F
3. God asks you to be responsible in the way you use your money.   T   F
4. Money should be a substitute for the values of family, love and justice. T   F
5. Respect for a person should be based on their economic importance.   T   F

Fill in the missing words in these sentences.

The Garcia family worked on their estimations for their family

(6) .... All the money earned was listed as

(7) .... The money given to the Church and to various

charitable organizations was entered as a (8) ....

The money used to pay for bills was listed as (9) ....

The money taken out of their paychecks and paid to the government

came under the listing of (10) ....

Working Together

Develop, as a class or at home as a family, a list of popular current TV shows. Discuss as a class the shows that serve the common good and those that neglect it. Give specific reasons for your choices.

Name...

Recalling Key Concepts

Complete the sentence using one word from the word bank.

CONCEPTION	MONEY	SACRED	HEALTH	INSTANT

1. From the moment of ...., you existed as a unique and sacred person.

2. Skipping practice to watch a movie is an example of .... gratification.

3. Participating in God's creation of a new human being is a .... act.

4. People are worthy of respect no matter what their age or condition of ....

5. A budget is a financial tool to aid in managing ....

Circle the T if the statement is true. Circle the F if the statement is false.

1. Every person is unique and is created in God's image and likeness.　　T　　F

2. The Church teaches that a sixth-grader is too young to bring goodness to others.　　T　　F

3. The Church welcomes children into its family through Baptism.　　T　　F

4. As we age, we become less valuable to society and to our families.　　T　　F

5. Money should be a substitute for the values of family, love and justice.　　T　　F

Name ....

Matching It Up

*One each line, write the letter of the description in Column B
that best goes with the term in Column A.*

A

B

1. .... Abortion

2. .... Common Good

3. .... Eternal Life

4. .... Heredity

5. .... Integrity

A. Refers to all the traits and characteristics a person inherits

B. Being true to the person you are

C. Ending the life of an unborn child

D. The promise to those who follow Jesus

E. The sum total needs of a given community to live

Working Together

In groups write a list of petitions for the whole class to offer in prayer as a way to contribute to the end of this year's learning.

Summary

We have learned about Family Life this year.

God's Gift of Family

- When I respect the traditions of my family, I show reverence for the diversity and variety that God created among all families.
- God has given me the responsibility to discern and use the gifts he has given me not only for my own good but also for the good of my family and the good of others.
- I am shaped by my family's history, customs and faith.

God's Gift of Self

- God invites me to accept a vocation to use my gifts and talents in a loving and good way.
- Determination takes courage of heart and is based on integrity, resilience and humility.
- Having goals gives direction in life; achieving goals requires hard work, patience and perseverance.

God's Gift of Life

- God wants the creation of new life to take place within the loving commitment of marriage.
- A child is a person and a blessing from God from the first moment of conception.
- Caring for a baby communicates love to the baby and a sense of belonging.

God's Gift of Love

- A modest person recognizes the sacredness of the body, guarding themselves as a treasure and seeing others in the same way.
- Good manners follow from an attitude of respect and enable us to shine as a child of God.
- Aging involves changes in every aspect of living, resulting in the joys and struggles of life.

God's Gift of Community

- The Catholic Church teaches that a society whose economic system subordinates a person to production or profits violates the person's dignity.
- Stewardship in the form of fiscal responsibility shows gratitude to God for the gifts and resources he provides for us.
- Each of us is responsible to support one another in working for the common good.

6

Recognition of Achievement

The faith community of

_____

proudly announces

_____

and family have completed the sixth level of
RCL Benziger Family Life.

This young person has discovered:
God's gift of family
God's gift of self
God's gift of life
God's gift of love
God's gift of community

May every day provide you and your family new adventures
in following Jesus and in living faithful Christian lives.

_____

(Signed)